Contents

Introduction 2
Beautiful and Profound Quotes 7
Short and Pithy Quotes 17
Inspirational and Uplifting Quotes 23
Oprah's Advice for Life 35
Wise and Enlightening Quotes 44
Quotes on God and Religion 50
Reflections, Opinions, and other Quotes 53

INTRODUCTION

Oprah Gail Winfrey was born to Vernita Lee and Vernon Winfrey on an isolated farm in Kosciusko, Mississippi, on January 29, 1954. Her name was supposed to be Orpah, from the Bible, but because of the difficulty of spelling and pronunciation, she was known as Oprah almost from birth. Winfrey's unmarried parents separated soon after she was born and left her in the care of her maternal grandmother on the farm.

As a child, Winfrey entertained herself by "playacting" in front of an "audience" of farm animals. Under the strict guidance of her grandmother, she learned to read at two and a half years old. She addressed her church congregation about "when Jesus rose on Easter Day" when she was two years old. Then Winfrey skipped kindergarten after writing a note to her teacher on the first day of school saying she belonged in the first grade. She was promoted to third grade after that year.

At six years old Winfrey was sent north to join her mother and two half-brothers in a Milwaukee ghetto, an extremely poor and dangerous neighborhood. At twelve years old she was sent to live with her father in Nashville, Tennessee. Feeling secure and happy for a brief period she began making speeches at social gatherings and churches, and one time earned five hundred dollars for a speech. She knew then that she wanted to be "paid to talk."

Winfrey, again, was called back by her mother, and she had to leave the safety of her father's home. The poor, urban lifestyle had its negative effect on Winfrey as a young teenager, and her problems were compounded by repeated sexual abuse, starting at age nine, by men that others in her family trusted. Her mother worked odd jobs and did not have much time for supervision.

After years of bad behavior, Winfrey's mother sent her back to her father in Nashville.

A turning point
Winfrey said her father saved her life. He was very strict and provided her with guidance, structure, rules, and books. He required his daughter to complete weekly book reports, and she went without dinner until she learned five new vocabulary words each day.

Winfrey became an excellent student, participating as well in the drama club, debate club, and student council. In an Elks Club speaking contest, she won a full scholarship to Tennessee State University. The following year she was invited to a White House Conference on Youth. Winfrey was crowned Miss Fire Prevention by WVOL, a local Nashville radio station, and was hired by the station to read afternoon newscasts.

Winfrey became Miss Black Nashville and Miss Tennessee during her freshman year at Tennessee State. The Nashville Columbia Broadcasting System (CBS) affiliate offered her a job; Winfrey turned it down twice, but finally took the advice of a speech teacher, who reminded her that job offers from CBS were "the reason people go to college." The show was seen each evening on WTVF-TV, and Winfrey was Nashville's first African American female coanchor of the evening news. She was nineteen years old and still a sophomore in college.

Professional career

After Winfrey graduated, WJZ-TV in Baltimore, Maryland, scheduled her to do the local news updates, called cut-ins, during Good Morning, America, and soon she was moved to the morning talk show Baltimore Is Talking with cohost Richard Sher. After seven years on the show, the general manager of WLS-TV, American Broadcasting Company's (ABC) Chicago affiliate, saw Winfrey in an audition tape sent in by her producer, Debra DiMaio. At the time her ratings in Baltimore were better than Phil Donahue's, a national talk-show host, and she and DiMaio were hired.

Winfrey moved to Chicago, Illinois, in January 1984 and took over as anchor on A.M. Chicago, a morning talk show that was consistently last in the ratings. She changed the emphasis of the show from traditional women's issues to current and controversial (debatable) topics, and after one month the show was even with Donahue's program. Three months later it had inched ahead. In September 1985 the program, renamed the Oprah Winfrey Show, was expanded to one hour. As a result, Donahue moved to New York City.

In 1985 Quincy Jones (1933–) saw Winfrey on television and thought she would make a fine actress in a movie he was coproducing with director Steven Spielberg (1946–). The film was based on the Alice Walker (1944–) novel The Color Purple. Her only acting experience until then had been in a one-woman show, The History of Black Women Through Drama and Song, which she performed during an African American theater festival in 1978.

Popularity of Oprah

The popularity of Winfrey's show skyrocketed after the success of The Color Purple, and in September 1985 the distributor King World bought the syndication rights (the rights to distribute a television program) to air the program in one hundred thirty-eight cities, a record for first-time syndication. That year, although Donahue was being aired on two hundred stations, Winfrey won her time slot by 31 percent, drew twice the Chicago audience as Donahue, and carried the top ten markets in the United States.

In 1986 Winfrey received a special award from the Chicago Academy for the Arts for unique contributions to the city's artistic community and was named Woman of Achievement by the National Organization of Women. The Oprah Winfrey Show won several Emmys for Best Talk Show, and Winfrey was honored as Best Talk Show Host.

Production

Winfrey formed her own production company, Harpo, Inc., in August 1986 to produce the topics that she wanted to see produced, including the television drama miniseries based on Gloria Naylor's The Women of Brewster Place, in which Winfrey was featured along with Cicely Tyson, Robin Givens, Olivia Cole, Jackee, Paula Kelly, and Lynn Whitfield. The miniseries aired in March 1989 and a regular series called Brewster Place, also starring Winfrey, debuted on ABC in May 1990. Winfrey also owned the screen rights to Kaffir Boy, Mark Mathabane's autobiographical (having to do with a story about oneself) book about growing up under apartheid in South Africa, as well as Toni Morrison's (1931–) novel Beloved.

In September 1996 Winfrey started an on-air reading club. On September 17 Winfrey stood up and announced she wanted "to get the country reading." She told her adoring fans to hasten to the stores to buy the book she had chosen. They would then discuss it together on the air the following month.

The initial reaction was astonishing. The Deep End of the Ocean had generated significant sales for a first novel; sixty-eight thousand copies had gone into the stores since June. But between the last week in August, when Winfrey told her plans to the publisher, and the September on-air announcement, Viking printed ninety thousand more. By the time the discussion was broadcast on October 18, there were seven hundred fifty thousand copies in print. The book became a number one best-seller, and another one hundred thousand were printed before February 1997.

The club ensured Winfrey as the most powerful book marketer in the United States. She sent more people to bookstores than morning news programs, other daytime shows, evening magazines, radio shows, print reviews, and feature articles combined. But after a six-year run with her book club, Winfrey decided to cut back in the spring of 2002 and no longer have the book club as a monthly feature.

The future

Although one of the wealthiest women in America and the highest paid entertainer in the world, Winfrey has made generous contributions to charitable organizations and institutions such as Morehouse College, the Harold Washington Library, the United Negro College Fund, and Tennessee State University.

*

Beautiful and Profound Quotes

Don't get confused with what people say you are, with who you know you are.

Even the wildest dreams have to start somewhere. Allow yourself the time and space to let your mind wander and your imagination fly.

When you have done everything that you can do, surrender. Give yourself up to the power and energy that's greater than yourself.

What I know for sure is that you feel real joy in direct proportion to how connected you are to living your truth.

Let excellence be your brand... When you are excellent, you become unforgettable. Doing the right thing, even when nobody knows you're doing the right thing will always bring the right thing to you.

The greatest discovery of all time is that a person can change his future by merely changing his attitude.

Oprah Fact: Winfrey was named "Orpah" after the biblical character in the Book of Ruth on her birth certificate, but people mispronounced it regularly and "Oprah" stuck.

You have to find what sparks a light in you so that you in your own way can illuminate the world.

I want to continue to encourage as many people as I can to open their hearts to life, because if I know anything for sure, it's that opening my own heart is what has brought me my greatest success and joy.

No matter where you are on your journey, that's exactly where you need to be. The next road is always ahead.

You cannot wait for someone to save you, to help you, to complete you. No one can complete you. You complete yourself.

The miracle of your existence calls for celebration every day.

The key to realizing a dream is to focus not on success but significance - and then even the small steps and little victories along your path will take on greater meaning.

Understand that the right to choose your own path is a sacred privilege. Use it. Dwell in possibility.

There is no greater gift you can give or receive than to honor your calling. It's why you were born. And how you become most truly alive.

Life is about becoming more of who you really are.

Oprah Fact: As a child, Oprah Winfrey was nicknamed "The Preacher" for her ability to recite Bible verses as her grandmother often took her to church.

What you focus on expands, and when you focus on the goodness in your life, you create more of it. Opportunities, relationships, even money flowed my way when I learned to be grateful no matter what happened in my life.

Knowing your deepest intention can be your guiding force in the creation of a better life.

Let your light shine. Shine within you so that it can shine on someone else. Let your light shine.

The more you praise and celebrate your life, the more there is in life to celebrate.

It makes no difference how many peaks you reach if there was no pleasure in the climb.

Move with the flow. Don't fight the current. Resist nothing. Let life carry you. Don't try to carry it.

When you don't know what to do, get still. The answer will come.

Your journey begins with a choice to get up, step out, and live fully.

I don't think of myself as a poor deprived ghetto girl who made good. I think of myself as somebody who from an early age knew I was responsible for myself, and I had to make good.

Oprah Fact: Winfrey was born the daughter of an unwed teen. Oprah's difficulties did not end with her childhood. She was sexually abused from age 9 to 13. At which point she ran away, and began to live a promiscuous life. She became a teenage mother at the mere age of 14, but motherhood was short lived. Her son died only two weeks later due to complications.

I'm finally ready to own my own power, to say, "This is who I am." If you like it, you like it. And if you don't like it, you don't. So watch out; I'm gonna fly.

Connect. Embrace. Liberate. Love somebody. Just one person. And then spread that to two. And as many as you can. You'll see the difference it makes.

My highest achievement: never shutting my heart down. Even in my darkest moments - through sexual abuse, a pregnancy at 14, lies and betrayals - I remained faithful, hopeful, and open to seeing the best in people, regardless of whether they were showing me their worst. I stayed open to believing that no matter how hard the climb, there is always a way to let in a sliver of light to illuminate the path forward.

What you focus on expands, and when you focus on the goodness in your life, you create more of it.

All of us need a vision for our lives, and even as we work to achieve that vision, we must surrender to the power that is greater than we know. It's one of the defining principles of my life that I love to share: God can dream a bigger dream for you than you could ever dream for yourself.

What God intended for you goes far beyond anything you can imagine.

I believe that every single event in life happens in an opportunity to choose love over fear.

Running is the greatest metaphor for life, because you get out of it what you put into it.

The single greatest thing you can do to change your life today would be to start being grateful for what you have right now. And the more grateful you are, the more you get.

Oprah Fact: At age 17, Winfrey won the Miss Black Tennessee beauty pageant.

I believe there's a calling for all of us. I know that every human being has value and purpose. The real work of our lives is to become aware. And awakened. To answer the call.

What matters is how you feel inside, because feeling beautiful on the inside is key to looking good.

Do what you have to do until you can do what you want to do.

Here's the gift of gratitude: In order to feel it, your ego has to take a backseat. What shows up in its place is greater compassion and understanding. Instead of being frustrated, you choose appreciation. And the more grateful you become, the more you have to be grateful for.

Be quiet. Part of your responsibility is to honour the quiet inside yourself so you can hear the call.

We are Spiritual Beings having a Human Experience. Not the other way around.

When I look into the future, it's so bright it burns my eyes.

We're all looking for the highest, fullest expression of ourselves as a human being.

When you surrender and stop resisting and stop trying to change that which you can't change, but be in the moment, be fully open to the blessings you've already received and those that are yet to come and stand in that space of gratitude ... and look at where you are and how far you've come and what you've accomplished - when you can claim that and see that, the literal vibration of your life will change.

The thing you fear most has no power. Your fear of it is what has the power. Facing the truth really will set you free.

My idea of heaven is a great big baked potato and someone to share it with.

Life whispers to you all the time...from the time you wake up in the morning and with every single experience.

With every experience, you alone are painting your own canvas, thought by thought, choice by choice.

I had no idea that being your authentic self could make me as rich as I've become. If I had, I'd have done it a lot earlier.

Oprah Fact: Oprah Winfrey is at least 8% Native American--something she discovered when undergoing a DNA test for the PBS show African American Lives.

Forgiveness is letting go of the hope that the past can be changed.

Bravery shows up in everyday life when people have the courage to live their truth, their vision and their dreams.

It is confidence in our bodies, minds and spirits that allows us to keep looking for new adventures.

That whisper you keep hearing is the universe trying to get your attention.

Living in the moment brings you a sense of reverence for all of life's blessings.

It isn't until you come to a spiritual understanding of who you are - not necessarily a religious feeling, but deep down, the spirit within - that you can begin to take control.

When people say they are looking for happiness, I ask, What are you giving to the world?

All life is energy and we are transmitting it at every moment. We are all little beaming little signals like radio frequencies, and the world is responding in kind.

I live in a space of thankfulness- And I have been rewarded a million times over for it. I started out giving thanks for the small things, and more thankful I become, the more my bounty increased, that's because what you focus on expands and when you focus on the goodness in your life, you create more of it.

If I lost control of the business I'd lose myself - or at least the ability to be myself. Owning myself is a way to be myself.

Appreciating what shows up in your life changes your personal vibration. Gratitude elevates your life to a higher frequency.

You want to be in the driver's seat of your own life because if you are not, life will drive you.

Your life is a journey of learning to love yourself first and then extending that love to others in every encounter.

Oprah Fact: Oprah Winfrey openly discussed her childhood sexual abuse suffered at the hands of male relatives and her mother's friends on a special episode of her show focusing on sexual abuse in 1986.

What material success does is provide you with the ability to concentrate on other things that really matter. And that is being able to make a difference, not only in your own life, but in other people's lives.

It's not easy being grateful all the time. But it's when you feel least thankful that you are most in need of what gratitude can give you.

Living in the moment means letting go of the past and not waiting for the future. It means living your life consciously, aware that each moment you breathe is a gift.

Allowing the truth of who you are-your spiritual self-to rule your life means you stop the struggle and learn to move with the flow of your life.

The choices we've made throughout our lives affect whatever happens to us in any given moment.

The whole point of being alive is to evolve into the complete person you were intended to be.

If you make a choice that doesn't please your mate, your friends, your mother, or whoever, the world will not fall apart - the people who truly love you want you to love yourself.

The essential question is not, "How busy are you?" but "What are you busy at?"

The way to choose happiness is to follow what is right and real and the truth for you.

We're all called. If you're here breathing, you have a contribution to make to our human community. The real work of your life is to figure out your function-your part in the whole-as soon as possible, and then get about the business of fulfilling it as only you can.

Oprah Fact: Oprah was anchoring the news at Nashville's WTVF-TV when she was just 19, making her the youngest person and the first African-American woman to hold the position.

You can either waltz boldly onto the stage of life and live the way you know your spirit is nudging you to, or you can sit quietly by the wall, receding into the shadows of fear and self doubt.

I want people to be more open and tolerant. I want them to know that behind every stranger is a backstory that is the common denominator - for we all share in the human experience: pain, sadness, grief, lack of love, and then, with hope and help, step by step achievements.

Balance lives in the present. The surest way to lose your footing is to focus on what dreadful things might happen.

What we're all striving for is authenticity, a spirit-to-spirit connection.

You can find the sacred in the most ordinary of things.

Oprah Fact: Since 1989, Oprah Winfrey says she has interviewed more than 37,000 people.

Short and Pithy Quotes

You get in life what you have the courage to ask for.

Never give up your power to another person.

True forgiveness is when you can say, 'Thank you for that experience.'

Listen. Pay attention. Treasure every moment.

One percent doubt is zero percent faith.

What I know for sure is that what you give comes back to you.

The greatest lesson of life is that you are responsible for your life.

Oprah Fact: Winfrey has donated her voice for an array cartoon characters, voicing Gussie the goose for Charlotte's Web, and Eudora, the mother of Princess Tiana in Disney's The Princess and the Frog, among others.

You are not your circumstances. You are your possibilities.

Anything you can imagine, you can create.

You become what you believe.

Living your best life is your most important journey in life.

I know for sure that what we dwell on is who we become.

I've learned not to worry about what might come next.

The happiness you feel is in direct proportion to the love you give.

Pray as if it's up to God, work as if it's up to you.

Be thankful for what you have; you'll end up having more.

Excellence is the best deterrent to racism or sexism.

You are built not to shrink down to less but to blossom into more.

Failure is a signpost to turn you in another direction.

No experience is ever wasted. Everything has meaning.

To love yourself is a never-ending journey.

Free speech not only lives, it rocks!

I always knew I was destined for greatness.

Happiness is there for the taking - and the making.

Oprah Fact: Oprah Winfrey has interviewed countless celebrities, including Michael Jackson, whose interview became the 4th most watched event in American television history, as well as the most watched interview of all-time, with 36 million viewers.

I believe that one of life's greatest risks is never daring to risk.

To move forward you have to give back.

When you undervalue what you do, the world will undervalue who you are.

No gesture is too small when done with gratitude.

All of life is energy and we are transmitting it at every moment.

You teach people how to treat you.

Doubt means don't. Don't move. Don't answer. Don't rush forward.

I always knew I was a hit record just waiting to happen.

Everybody's life matters.

Everyone has to learn to think differently, bigger, to open to possibilities.

Luck is a matter of preparation meeting opportunity.

Doing the best at this moment puts you in the best place for the next moment.

Biology is the least of what makes someone a mother.

Your true passion should feel like breathing; it's that natural.

When you learn to say thank you, you see the world anew.

Trust your instincts. Intuition doesn't lie.

You get to know who you really are in a crisis.

Live from the heart of yourself.

The next road is always ahead.

You get from the world what you give to the world.

Tithe in kind where your spirit is fed.

Oprah Fact: Winfrey credits her grandmother for guiding her towards success, saying that it was Hattie Mae who encouraged her to speak up in public, giving Winfrey confidence at an early age and a positive sense of self.

Always listen to your inner voice.

Ordinary people can bring about change.

You have to be responsible for the energy you're putting out into the world.

Skiing is the next best thing to having wings.

Don't live your life to please other people.

All stress comes from resisting what is.

I don't want anyone who doesn't want me.

The best of times is now.

Everyone is the keeper of a dream.

When people show you who they are ... believe them!

There's nothing worse than betraying yourself.

Oprah Fact: Winfrey was nominated for an Academy Award for Best Supporting Actress for her role in Steven Spielberg's The Color Purple.

Inspirational and Uplifting Quotes

Create the highest, grandest vision possible for your life, because you become what you believe.

You will be wounded many times in your life. You'll make mistakes. Some people will call them failures but I have learned that failure is really God's way of saying, "Excuse me, you're moving in the wrong direction." It's just an experience, just an experience.

You don't become what you want, you become what you believe.

Whenever I'm faced with a difficult decision, I ask myself, 'What would I do if I weren't afraid of making a mistake? Feeling rejected? looking foolish? Or being alone?' I know for sure that when you remove the fear, the answer that you've been searching for comes into focus and as you walk into your fear, you should know for sure that your deepest struggle can, if you're willing and open, produce your greatest strength.

Failure is a great teacher and, if you are open to it, every mistake has a lesson to offer.

Oprah Fact: Winfrey is credited for popularizing the intimate, confessional form of talk show, which has since become common across cable networks. She was instrumental in launching Oxygen Media, dedicated to producing cable programming specifically for women.

I trust that everything happens for a reason, even if we are not wise enough to see it.

What I know for sure is this: The big secret in life is that there is no big secret. Whatever your goal for this year is, you can get there - as long as you're willing to be honest with yourself about the preparation and work involved. There are no back doors, no free rides. There's just you, this moment, and a choice.

Learn from every mistake because every experience, encounter, and particularly your mistakes are there to teach you and force you into being more who you are.

If you're sitting around waiting on somebody to save you, to fix you, to even help you, you are wasting your time because only you have the power to take responsibility to move your life forward.

You've got to follow your passion. You've got to figure out what it is you love--who you really are. And have the courage to do that. I believe that the only courage anybody ever needs is the courage to follow your own dreams.

With every failure, every crisis, every difficult time, I say - What is this here to teach me? And as soon as you get the lesson, you get to move on. If you really get the lesson, you pass and you don't have to repeat the class.

My philosophy is that not only are you responsible for your life, but doing the best at this moment puts you in the best place for the next moment.

No experience is wasted. Everything in life is happening to grow you up, to fill you up, to help you become more of who you were created to be.

Whatever you fear most has no power - it is your fear that has the power. The thing itself cannot touch you. But if you allow your fear to seep into your mind and overtake your thoughts, it will rob you of your life.

I am a woman in process. I'm just trying like everybody else. I try to take every conflict, every experience, and learn from it. Life is never dull.

Oprah Fact: In 2013, Winfrey was awarded the Presidential Medal of Freedom (the nation's highest civilian honor) by President Barack Obama.

If you are still breathing, you have a second chance.

I've come to believe that each of us has a personal calling that's as unique as a fingerprint - and that the best way to succeed is to discover what you love and then find a way to offer it to others in the form of service, working hard, and also allowing the energy of the universe to lead you.

You define your own life. Don't let other people write your script.

Nobody's journey is seamless or smooth. We all stumble. We all have setbacks. It's just life's way of saying, 'Time to change course.'

Turn your wounds into wisdom.

Whatever someone did to you in the past has no power over the present. Only you give it power.

You only have to believe that you can succeed, that you can be whatever your heart desires, be willing to work for it, and you can have it.

Do the one thing you think you cannot do. Fail at it. Try again. Do better the second time. The only people who never tumble are those who never mount the high wire. This is your moment. Own it.

I trust in the ebb and flow of the universe. I trust that life's bigger than what I can see. I trust that there is a divine order beyond my control. And I trust that no matter what happens, I will be all right.

Follow your passion. It will lead you to your purpose.

Every day brings a chance to live free of regret and with as much joy, fun, and laughter as you can stand.

The biggest adventure you can take is to live the life of your dreams.

I don't believe in failure. It is not failure if you enjoyed the process.

I was once afraid of people saying, "Who does she think she is?" Now I have the courage to stand and say, "This is who I am."

Oprah Fact: Oprah Winfrey has reached a completely new level of success. The 59-year-old African-American woman is the only person to have been listed in Time magazine's 100 most influential people nine times. She is also the first African American woman to appear on Forbes billionaire list. She has also been considered one of the most influential people in the world.

The only courage you will need is the courage to live the life you are meant to.

We often block our own blessings because we don't feel inherently good enough or smart enough or pretty enough or worthy enough... You're worthy because you are born and because you are here. Your being here, your being alive makes worthiness your birthright. You alone are enough.

Forgiveness is giving up the hope that the past could have been any different, it's accepting the past for what it was, and using this moment and this time to help yourself move forward.

Life is full of many unpredictable changes... Let go of chaos yesterday; cheerfully live for today, and look forward to tomorrow with greater possibilities... It's our imperfections that make us perfect in our own unique ways.

It's all about dreams. If I had to attribute my success in life to any one thing it is this. I believed in my dreams, even when no one else did.

You are not the product of your circumstances. You are a composite of all the things you believe, and all the places you believe you can go. Your past does not define you. You can step out of your history and create a new day for yourself. Even if the entire culture is saying, "You can't." Even if every single possible bad thing that can happen to you does. You can keep going forward.

Where there is no struggle, there is no strength.

It doesn't matter how far you might rise. At some point you are bound to stumble because if you're constantly doing what we do, raising the bar. If you're constantly pushing yourself higher, higher the law of averages not to mention the Myth of Icarus predicts that you will at some point fall. And when you do I want you to know this, remember this: there is no such thing as failure. Failure is just life trying to move us in another direction.

You become what you believe. You are where you are today in your life based on everything you have believed.

When you live with an open heart, unexpected, joyful things happen.

You do what you have to do to get through today, and that puts you in the best place tomorrow.

Self-esteem means knowing you are the dream.

Oprah Fact: Her show, The Oprah Winfrey Show, also simply known as Oprah, won the Daytime Emmy Awards 47 times. Oprah's ultra-successful show would have most likely won more, but in 2000, Oprah decided to remove her show from being considered for any future Emmys.

What I know for sure: Often we don't even realize who we're meant to be because we're so busy trying to live out someone else's ideas. But other people and their opinions hold no power in defining our destiny.

You need to dream a bigger dream for yourself. That is the lesson. Hold the highest vision possible for your life and it can come true.

You become what you believe - not what you wish or want but what you truly believe. Wherever you are in life, look at your beliefs. They put you there.

When you're doing the work you're meant to do, it feels right and every day is a bonus, regardless of what you're getting paid.

You face the biggest challenge of all: to have the courage to seek your big dream regardless of what anyone says. You are the only person alive who can see your big picture and even you can't see it all.

Right now you are one choice away from a new beginning - one that leads you toward becoming the fullest human being you can be.

Be more splendid, more extraordinary. Use every moment to fill yourself up.

What I know for sure is that behind every catastrophe, there are great lessons to be learned. Among the many that we as a country need to get is that as long as we play the "us and them" game, we don't evolve as people, as a nation, as a planet.

Lessons often come dressed up as detours and roadblocks.

People never fail to amaze me. They face the unimaginable with a shot of grace and a rush of adrenaline; they steel their nerves; they summon their cool or anger or faith or whatever it takes to pull them through, and they go on to live another day.

Would you do your job and not be paid for it? I would do this job, and take on a second job just to make ends meet if nobody paid me. That's how you know you are doing the right thing.

I want every day to be a fresh start on expanding what is possible.

The only people who never tumble are those who never mount the high wire.

To come from no voice, no power, and to be able to achieve what I have means that only my own personal vision holds me back.

The only thing that can free you is the belief that you can be free.

Oprah Fact: Oprah had a very difficult childhood. As a young girl, she lived with her grandmother for some time, and they were so poor that Oprah would wear potato sack dresses. Her dolls were made from cornhusks. Her first pair of shoes graced her feet on her sixth birthday.

All my life I have always known I was born to greatness.

I know for sure that appreciating whatever shows up for you in life changes your personal vibration. You radiate and generate more goodness for yourself when you're aware of all you have and not focusing on your have-nots.

Whatever our dreams, ideas, or projects, we plant a seed, nurture it -- and then reap the fruits of our labors.

If we're really committed to growth, we never stop discovering new dimensions of self and self-expression .

Right now you are one choice away from a new beginning.

I will just create, and if it works, it works, and if it doesn't, I'll create something else. I don't have any limitations on what I think I could do or be.

Have the courage to follow your passion - and if you don't know what it is, realize that one reason for your existence on earth is to find it.

You become what you believe. And to believe that you are created by the power that's greater than yourself means anything is possible.

Don't waste your time in the race looking back to see what the other guy is doing. It's not about the other guy. It's about what can you do. You just need to run that race as hard as you can. You need to give it everything you've got, all the time, for yourself.

The way through the challenge is to get still and ask yourself, 'What is the next right move? What is the next right move?' and then, from that space, make the next right move and the next right move.

Difficulties come when you don't pay attention to life's whisper. Life always whispers to you first, but if you ignore the whisper, sooner or later you'll get a scream.

Year's end is neither an end nor a beginning but a going on, with all the wisdom that experience can instill in us. Cheers to a new year and another chance for us to get it right.

It's up to each of us to get very still and say, 'This is who I am.' No one else defines your life. Only you do.

You become what you believe, not what you think or what you want.

Every time you state what you want or believe, you're the first to hear it. It's a message to both you and others about what you think is possible. Don't put a ceiling on yourself.

Dream the biggest dream for yourself. Hold the highest vision of life for yourself.

Your mistake does not define who you are...you are your possibilities.

Oprah Fact: She was a gifted child. Her grandmother and father encouraged her education. Her grandmother taught her to read early on, and by the age of 2 ½, Oprah could read. In school, she was always put ahead of her class, and advanced to third grade once she had completed first grade.

Follow your instincts. That's where true wisdom manifests itself.

Every one of us gets through the tough times because somebody is there, standing in the gap to close it for us.

What I know for sure is this: You are built not to shrink down to less, but to blossom into more. To be more extraordinary. To use every moment to fill yourself up.

Your life is big. Keep reaching.

I am where I am because of the bridges I have crossed.

Every time a child is saved from the dark side of life, every time one of us makes the effort to make a difference in a child's life, we add light and healing to our own lives.

Challenges are gifts that force us to search for a new center of gravity. Don't fight them. Just find a new way to stand.

The true test of courage is to be afraid and to go ahead and do it anyway - to be scared, is to have your knees knocking, but to walk on in there anyway.

Find the courage to seek out your big dream, regardless of what anyone else says or thinks.

Don't complain about what you don't have. Use what you've got. To be less than your best is a sin.

Every day brings a chance for you to draw in a breath, kick off your shoes, and dance.

Honor your calling. Everybody has one. Trust your heart and success will come to you.

Oprah Fact: Her globally famous television show, The Oprah Winfrey Show, has successfully aired from 1986 to 2011. This television show changed the world of talk shows. Her show was an immediate success.

She replaced Phil Donahue, whose show was the most watched daytime talk shows in America.

What you believe has more power than what you dream or wish or hope for. You become what you believe.

Every birthday, you decide whether to mark it the end of your greatest days or the beginning of your finest hour.

I choose to rise up out of that storm and see that in moments of desperation, fear, and helplessness, each of us can be a rainbow of hope, doing what we can to extend ourselves in kindness and grace to one another. And I know for sure that there is no them - there's only us.

It doesn't take a lot to make me happy. I take pleasure from everything I do.

Oprah's Advice for Life

You are responsible for your life. You can't keep blaming somebody else for your dysfunction. Life is really about moving on.

Always take a stand for yourself, your values. You're defined by what you stand for.

If friends disappoint you over and over, that's in large part your own fault. Once someone has shown a tendency to be self-centered, you need to recognize that and take care of yourself; people aren't going to change simply because you want them to.

Oprah Fact: People loved Oprah immediately. Her way of interacting with her guests became labeled as, 'Oprahfication', a word that has now been added to the dictionary as well. It is defined as a means of discussing ones emotional problems through public disclosure. Oprah would cry with her guests on live TV as they shared their problems. According to Time magazine, "She makes people care because she cares."

Surround yourself with only people who are going to lift you higher.

If you don't heal the wounds of your childhood, you bleed into the future.

Nobody but you is responsible for your life. You are responsible for your life. What is your life? What is all life? What is every flower, every rock, every tree? Energy. And you're responsible for the energy you create for yourself, and you're responsible for the energy that you bring to others.

Follow your feelings. If it feels right, move forward. If it doesn't feel right, don't do it.

Find a way to get paid for doing what you love. Then every paycheck will be a bonus.

We have to steer our true life's course. Whatever your calling is in life! The whole purpose of being here is to figure out what that is as soon as possible, so you go about the business of being on track, of not being owned by what your mother said, what society said, whatever people think a woman is supposed to be when you can exceed other people's expectations and be defined by your own!

Worrying is wasted time. Use the same energy for doing something about whatever worries you.

Real integrity is doing the right thing, knowing that nobody's going to know whether you did it or not.

If it doesn't feel right, don't do it. That is the lesson, and that lesson alone will save you a lot of grief.

How do I define success? Let me tell you, money's pretty nice. But having a lot of money does not automatically make you a successful person. What you want is money and meaning. You want your work to be meaningful, because meaning is what brings the real richness to your life.

Passion is energy. Feel the power that comes from focusing on what excites you.

As you become more clear about who you really are, you'll be better able to decide what is best for you - the first time around.

I was raised to believe that excellence is the best deterrent to racism or sexism. And that's how I operate my life.

The key is not to worry about being successful, but to instead to work toward being significant - and the success will naturally follow.

One of the biggest lessons I've learned recently is that when you don't know what to do, you should do nothing until you figure out what to do because a lot of times you feel like you are pressed against the wall, and you've got to make a decision. You never have to do anything. Don't know what to do? Do nothing.

Breathe. Let go. And remind yourself that this very moment is the only one you know you have for sure.

You can't do it all yourself. Don't be afraid to rely on others to help you accomplish your goals.

Before you agree to do anything that might add even the smallest amount of stress to your life, ask yourself: What is my truest intention? Give yourself time to let a yes resound within you. When it's right, I guarantee that your entire body will feel it.

Oprah Fact: After a tumultuous beginning, Oprah began to get back on her feet. She had great success in school, and was an honor student in high school. She received a full scholarship to attend Tennessee State

University, where she graduated with a degree in Speech and Performing Arts.

I've always known that life is better when you share it. I now realize it gets even sweeter when you expand the circle.

Check your ego at the door and check your gut instead. Every right decision I have ever made has come from my gut. Every wrong decision I've made was the result of me not listening to the greater voice of myself.

I finally realized that being grateful to my body was key to giving more love to myself.

If a man wants you, nothing can keep him away,If he doesn't want you, nothing can make him stay. Stop making excuses for a man and his behavior. Stop trying to change yourself for a relationship that's not meant to be.

Slower is better. Never live your life for a man before you find what makes you truly happy.

What I know is, if you do work that you love, and work that fulfills you, the rest will come. I truly believe the reason I've been so financially successful is because my focus has never been on the money.

Committing to a lifetime of wellness is not a luxury-it's a necessity. You'll never have enough time; you have to make the time.

I urge you to pursue preserving your personal history to allow your children and grandchildren to know who you were as a child and what your hopes and dreams were.

If a man wants you, nothing can keep him away. If he doesn't want you, nothing can make him stay.

The great courageous act that we must all do, is to have the courage to step out of our history and past so that we can live our dreams.

Don't wait for someone else to complete you. 'Jerry Maguire' was just a movie.

Keeping a journal will change your life in ways that you'd never imagine.

One of my best moves is to surround myself with friends who, instead of asking, 'Why?' are quick to say, 'Why not?' That attitude is contagious.

Oprah Fact: Oprah's philanthropy work knows no boundaries. She has provided more than 400 students with scholarships. She is known for spending luxurious amounts of money on vacation trips that she enjoys with staff, friends and family. Oprah's Angel Network raised US$ 80 million for national and international non-profit organizations. During natural disasters such as Hurricane Katrina, Oprah donated US$ 10 million to help survivors get back on their feet. She has worked hard with the poor children of South Africa, donating US$ 40 million to help build schools for girls. As of 2012, she has donated approximately US$ 400 million to educational charities.

The big secret in life is there is no secret. Whatever your goal. You can get there if you're willing to work.

Forget about the fast lane. If you really want to fly, just harness your power to your passion.

You look at yourself and you accept yourself for who you are, and once you accept yourself for who you are you become a better person.

If you neglect to recharge a battery, it dies. And if you run full speed ahead without stopping for water, you lose momentum to finish the race.

If you're hurting, you need to help somebody else ease their hurt. If you're in pain, help somebody else's pain.

Think about any attachments that are depleting your emotional reserves. Consider letting them go.

Meditate. Breathe consciously. Listen. Pay attention. Treasure every moment. Make the connection.

The smallest change in perspective can transform a life. What tiny attitude adjustment might turn your world around?

The greatest contribution you can make to women's rights, is to be the absolute ... best at what you do.

Oprah Fact: She was originally named Orpah Gail Winfrey by her biological aunt, a word found in the Bible, which was also recorded on her birth certificate. Due to misspellings and mispronunciations, she decided to change her name to Oprah, the household name we all know of today.

You can't accomplish anything worthwhile if you inhibit yourself. If life teaches you nothing else, know this for sure: When you get the chance, go for it.

The best way to look at aging is to see it as an opportunity to leave what didn't work behind and step boldly into a brand new future.

Always keep your words soft and sweet, just in case you'll have to eat them, you can swallow it well.

When you don't give yourself the time and care you need, your body rebels in the form of sickness and exhaustion.

Use what you have to run toward your best - that's how I now live my life.

Partake of some of life's sweet pleasures. And yes, get comfortable with yourself.

Improving your life doesn't have to be about changing everything – it's about making changes that count.

So, that is my final lesson from the universe - you just do what you need to do, and stay on track.

Only make decisions that support your self-image, self-esteem, and self-worth.

Keep a grateful journal. Every night, list five things that you are grateful for. What it will begin to do is change our perspective of your day and your life.

Devote today to something so daring even you can't believe you're doing it.

Keep a grateful journal. Every night, list five things that happened this day that you are grateful for. What it will begin to do is change your perspective of your day and your life. If you can learn to focus on what you have, you will always see that the universe is abundant; you will have more. If you concentrate on what you don't have, you will never have enough.

Oprah Fact: Oprah has had a series of relationships throughout her life, but the one that did not get away is the lucky man, Stedman Graham. They have been in a relationship since 1986, and remain together to this day. In 1992, they planned a possible wedding, but did not go through with it.

If you want to feel good, you have to go out and do some good.

You will survive anything if you live your life from the point of view of truth.

Start embracing the life that is calling you and use your life to serve the world.

Do not waste your time with people who have shown you they really mean no good for you.

Eating more consciously now feels like a way of being. I actually think about how my food got to my plate.

Waking up early on Saturday gives me an edge in finishing my work with a very relaxed state of mind. There is a feeling of time pressure on weekdays that aren't there on weekends. If I wake up early in the morning before anybody else, I can plan the day or at least my activities with relaxed mind.

Wise and Enlightening Quotes

Be thankful for what you have; you'll end up having more. If you concentrate on what you don't have, you will never, ever have enough.

Leadership is about empathy. It is about having the ability to relate to and connect with people for the purpose of inspiring and empowering their lives.

There is no paycheck that can equal the feeling of contentment that comes from being the person you are meant to be.

The key to realizing a dream is to focus not on success but significance.

If you look at what you have in life, you'll always have more. If you look at what you don't have in life, you'll never have enough.

Oprah Fact: Oprah is a multitalented individual who can be successful at anything she puts her mind to. In 1985, she starred in the infamous movie, The Color Purple. Her talent was appreciated by a nomination for an Academy Award for Best Supporting Actress. She has since starred in other films and has been the voice for many characters of animated films.

You CAN have it all. You just can't have it all at once.

Everybody has a story. And there's something to be learned from every experience.

Anybody pretending to be anything other than who you really are- you will never, ever reach your personal potential.

Every choice gives you a chance to pave your own road. Keep moving. Full speed ahead.

The best way to succeed is to discover what you love and find a way to offer it to others.

Every choice in life either moves you forward or keeps you stuck.

What I learned at a very early age was that I was responsible for my life. And as I became more spiritually conscious, I learned that we all are responsible for ourselves, that you create your own reality by the way you think and therefore act. You cannot blame your parents, your circumstances, because you are NOT your circumstances. You are your possibilities. If you know that, you can do anything.

Nothing is ever wrong. We learn from every step we take. Whatever you did today was the way it was meant to be. Be proud of you.

Purpose is the thread that connects the dots to everything you do that leads you to an extraordinary life.

Your calling isn't something that somebody can tell you about. It's what you feel. It is the thing that gives you juice. The thing that you are supposed to do. And nobody can tell you what that is. You know it inside yourself.

If you want to accomplish the goals of your life, you have to begin with the spirit.

No matter who you are, no matter what your culture is, it is absolutely possible to look out and extend yourself in such a way, that you can connect to other people and find that we are more alike than we are different.

When you choose the paradigm of service, it turns everything you do from a job into a gift.

Oprah Fact: She has been criticized for her lavish expenditures. She owns multiple homes located all over North and South America and has a closet the size of an average apartment. However, her favorite car is the Volkswagen Beetle.

We're all called. If you're here breathing, you have a contribution to make.

You cannot be loving when you are blaming. You cannot be loving when you are criticizing. You cannot be loving when you are judging.

True self-esteem is realizing that you are valuable because you were born. No matter where you came from, what color your skin is, what people say about your family or what mean things people may have done to you, because you were born, you are important and you matter.

You know you are on the road to success if you would do your job, and not be paid for it.

Inner wisdom is more important than wealth. The more you spend it, the more you gain.

There is no such thing as failure. Failure is just life trying to move us in another direction.

I've learned that you can't have everything and do everything at the same time.

One if the hardest things in life to learn are which bridges to cross and which bridges to burn.

Unless you choose to do great things with it, it makes no difference how much you are rewarded, or how much power you have.

If you come to fame not understanding who you are, it will define who you are.

Truth allows you to live with integrity. Everything you do and say shows the world who you really are. Let it be the Truth.

Real success means creating a life of meaning through service that fulfills your reason for being here.

Oprah Fact: Oprah's show was not her only success. In 2000, she launched the much-awaited monthly magazine, O: The Oprah Magazine. In 2009, she created her own network, The Oprah Winfrey Network. During the days of her talk show, she also launched Oprah's Book Club, which since 1996 has listed 65 books.

I don't believe in luck. Luck is just preparation meeting the moment of opportunity.

A lesson will keep repeating itself until it is learned. Life first will send the lesson to you in the size of a pebble; if you ignore the pebble, then life will send you a brick; if you ignore the brick, life will send you a brick wall; if you ignore the brick wall, life will send you a demolition truck.

The way to choose happiness is to follow what is right and real and the truth for you. You can never be happy living someone else's dream. Live your own. And you will for sure know the meaning of happiness.

Our beliefs can move us forward in life, or they can hold us back.

The roles we play in each other's lives are only as powerful as the trust and connection between us--the protection, safety, and caring we are willing to share.

In order to be truly happy, you must live along with, and you must stand for something larger than yourself.

Become the change you want to see - those are words I live by.

I still want what I've always wanted ... to be the best person I can be.

Self-esteem comes from being able to define the world in your own terms and refusing to abide by the judgments of others.

That's really what wealth does for you. It gives you freedom to make choices.

There's a wealth that has nothing to do with dollars, that comes from the perspective and wisdom of paying attention to your life.

Opportunity may knock only once but temptation leans on the door bell.

I believe luck is preparation meeting opportunity. If you hadn't been prepared when the opportunity came along, you wouldn't have been lucky.

It's only when you make the process your goal that the big dream can follow.

Oprah Fact: Oprah has made history for women and black people alike. For three years, 2004-2006, Forbes magazine listed Oprah Winfrey as the world's only black billionaire. She is also the first black woman billion in the world. Oprah is also now the richest woman entrepreneur in America, moving Meg Whitman, previous CEO of eBay down the list.

If you come to fame not understanding who you are, it will define who you are. It shouldn't change you. If you're a jerk, you just get to be a bigger jerk. What fame does is magnify who you are and puts that on a platter for the whole world to see.

Do what you want to do, when you want to do it ... and not a moment sooner.

How you spend your time defines who you are.

Quotes on God and Religion

I hear people say all the time, "I'm not really religious, but I consider myself spiritual." I definitely have always been spiritual, being raised by my grandmother on that little acre in Mississippi, indoctrinated, born into the church and the ways of the church.

God is a feeling experience and not a believing experience. If your religion is a believing experience ... then that's not truly God.

I can't define "God," so to be open to the mystical and mystery of God is a natural part of myself. So people criticize me for not being what they are, and I say, it's working for me and has worked for me and continues to work for me, in a way that fills me with a sense of peace and contentment about what God means to me.

Oprah Fact: Many question why Oprah did not try to become a mother again. Her loving attitude and selfless devotion would have made her a wonderful mother. When asked, Oprah stated that she would never want to be a mother because of her own neglected childhood. Oprah's mother was not the ideal mother, and Oprah was the one who had to suffer for her mistakes.

In God, I move and breathe and have my being.

What other people label or might try to call failure, I have learned is just God's way of pointing you in a new direction.

Well, I am a Christian who believes that there are certainly many more paths to God other than Christianity.

God can dream a bigger dream for you than you can dream for yourself, and your role on Earth is to attach yourself to that divine force and let yourself be released to it.

I was like you are. I thought Jesus came and died on the cross. Jesus' being here was about his death and dying on the cross but it really was about him coming to show us how to do it. To show us the Christ-consciousness that he had and that consciousness abides in all of us. That's what I got. That's what I got.

I am extremely spiritual. I've not gone into this before because it's personal, but faith is the core of my life.

One of the biggest mistakes humans make is to believe there is only one way. There are many diverse paths leading to what you call God.

Oprah Fact: Oprah is a great advocate of self-help and spirituality. She has co-authored five books, which have all been successful, through the support of her book club. Her books range from cookbooks, to spiritual self-help books to books about how to lose weight. In 2005, Oprah announced the upcoming launch of a new weight loss book. She received a book advance fee, which has been said to be the world's highest, surpassing even Bill Clinton's book advance fee for his autobiography.

I live inside God's dream for me. I don't try to tell God what I'm supposed to do. . . God can dream a bigger dream for you than you can dream for yourself.

The nature of Buddhism, as I understand it, is to believe that we are all pure and radiant at our core. And yet we see around us so much evidence that people are not acting from a place of purity and radiance.

I'm definitely not a traditionalist, because a traditionalist would be going to church every Sunday.

Reflections, Opinions, and other Quotes

Lots of people want to ride with you in the limo, but what you want is someone who will take the bus with you when the limo breaks down.

Don't settle for a relationship that won't let you be yourself.

The stories that you tell yourself can make or break you - no matter who you are.

I am grateful for the blessings of wealth, but it hasn't changed who I am. My feet are still on the ground. I'm just wearing better shoes.

My name is Oprah Winfrey. I have a talk show. I'm single. I have eight dogs-five golden retrievers, two black labs, and a mongrel. I have four years of college.

Oprah Fact: Oprah's best friend is Gayle King. The two have been friends since 1976. Gayle is currently the editor of Oprah's magazine, O: The Oprah Magazine. In 2008, Oprah bought her best friend a penthouse located in New York City worth US$ 7.1 million. There have been rumors regarding the two women's friendship, which Oprah has waved off, and promised to inform the public of any such relationship down the road.

I think education is power. I think that being able to communicate with people is power. One of my main goals on the planet is to encourage people to empower themselves.

There is a seeded bread that I bring from South Africa. I bring home

10, 20 loaves. I am so bad with this bread. I've literally been in hotels and brought my own: "Please, can you toast this? I have my own bread." They're like, "You have your own bread?" And I'll pull it out!

Getting my library card was like citizenship; it was like American citizenship.

If I had kids, my kids would hate me. They would have ended up on the equivalent of the Oprah show talking about me; because something [in my life] would have had to suffer and it would've probably been them.

The struggle of my life created empathy... I could relate to pain... being abandoned... having people not love me.

I became so frustrated with visiting inner-city schools (in America) that I just stopped going. The sense that you need to learn just isn't there. If you ask the kids what they want or need, they will say an iPod or some sneakers. In South Africa, they don't ask for money or toys. They ask for uniforms so they can go to school.

What dogs? These are my children, little people with fur who make my heart open a little wider.

Dogs are my favorite role models. I want to work like a dog, doing what I was born to do with joy and purpose. I want to play like a dog, with total, jolly abandon. I want to love like a dog, with unabashed devotion and complete lack of concern about what people do for a living, how much money they have, or how much they weigh. The fact that we still live with dogs, even when we don't have to herd or hunt our dinner, gives me hope for humans and canines alike.

Education is the way to move mountains, to build bridges, to change the world. Education is the path to the future. I believe that education is indeed freedom.

My first day in Chicago, September 4, 1983. I set foot in this city, and just walking down the street, it was like roots, like the motherland. I knew I belonged here.

I'm starting to cry. I'm remembering those years I struggled with my weight, those times when I saw my reflection in a store window and didn't know who that fat person was, years when it was a big accomplishment for me to exercise at two dots on the StairMaster. And now I'm finishing a 26-mile race. Damn! This is better than winning an Emmy!

Oprah Fact: Oprah has always been proud of her figure. She revolutionized the television world with her confessions about her weight, which made it easier for other overweight women such as Rosie O'Donnell, to be accepted on screen. Oprah's weight reached a maximum of 238 lbs., after which she lost 90 lbs., reaching her ideal weight of 150 lbs.

Books were my pass to personal freedom. I learned to read at age three, and soon discovered there was a whole world to conquer that went beyond our farm in Mississippi.

You must feed your mind with reading material, thoughts, and ideas that open you to new possibilities.

I can't deny that Jerry Springer supposedly beating us didn't affect me. There was a point where I felt like, Golly, you work so hard, you try so hard and the people say they want meaningful television and then Jerry Springer ends up beating you. It was disturbing.

I'm always interested in people being able to share stories that allow us to see the landscape of human foibles, challenges, and ultimately triumph.

This past Thanksgiving, my father was at the farm, and I had all 11 dogs in the house with a father who never allowed dogs in the house. And he got up to leave the table and came back and Solomon was in his chair. And he says, "This dog is in my chair." And I said, "It's the other way around, you're sitting in his chair."

Some women have a weakness for shoes... I can go barefoot if necessary. I have a weakness for books.

I have crossed over on the backs of Sojourner Truth, Harriet Tubman, Fannie Lou Hamer, and Madam C. J. Walker. Because of them I can now live the dream. I am the seed of the free, and I know it. I intend to bear great fruit.

My first deepening of spirituality came when I was 6, when I was moved from my grandmother and sent to live with my mother - whom I really did not know - who had moved to Milwaukee. Something inside myself knew that I was never going to see my grandmother again - I would be wasting my time to live in that space of wanting that.

Oprah Fact: Oprah has always been an entertainer. Even when she was a poverty-stricken young girl, she found ways to be on stage. Her grandmother said that she would interview her cornhusk doll amidst the crows that would hang around their house. Oprah has a natural talent of finding beauty even in adversity.

Education is the key to unlocking the world, a passport to freedom.

Is it shocking that it's very difficult for a news organization to do news in America now? It's not shocking because we're a culture that doesn't want news. We want entertainment. We want info-tainment. That's why CNN is having problems.

I love hearing stories, telling stories, sharing stories. I've shared 37,000 on the Oprah show! Every day I was like the town crier.

Made in the USA
Middletown, DE
22 December 2020